DEVELOPING A NONPROFIT BUSINESS

*Planning Fundable Programs and Services That
Entice Grantors and Community Sponsors*

Robin Devereaux-Nelson

Table of Contents

CHAPTER 1: 1

What Does "Nonprofit" Mean 1

Nonprofit Classification 1

Nonprofit Regulation 2

Acquiring a DUNS Number 2

CHAPTER 2: 4

Steps to Becoming a Nonprofit Business 4

Developing a Business Plan 6

Federal Application for 501c3 Nonprofit Status 11

License to Solicit Charitable Funds 12

CHAPTER 3: 13

Developing Programs and Services 13

Consider Your Potential Consumers 15

Community Partners 16

CHAPTER 4: 17

Applying for Grants – A Brief Overview 17

Application Types 17

Parts of a Grant 17

Required Attachments 20

Drafting the Cover Letter 21

CHAPTER 5: 22

What Do Grantors Look For? 22

CHAPTER 6: 25

Seeking Corporate Sponsorships 25

CHAPTER 7: 27

Steps to Hosting A Successful Annual Campaign 27

CHAPTER 8: 32

Conducting an Annual Nonprofit Campaign 32

CHAPTER 9: 39

Using Social Networking Technologies in Your
Nonprofit Organization 39

CHAPTER 10: 43

Social Networking for Nonprofit Organizations 43

CHAPTER 11: 49

Planning a Special Nonprofit Event 49

CHAPTER 12: 53

Board Recruitment for Nonprofit Organizations........ 53

Conclusion... 56

Introduction

Nonprofit organizations exist in communities to aid or assist many types of populations. There are more than 1.5 million not for profit corporations in the United States alone, according to the Foundation Center. A nonprofit corporation should be managed and operated like any other business; however, since they are public entities and have gained a tax-exempt status from the government, they must adhere to some specific rules and guidelines.

Nonprofit corporations generally rely heavily on grant and corporate funding, so it is important when developing a nonprofit organization to make sure its programs and services are designed to attract funders. This means a program that delivers an excellent product, is managed well, is financially sound, has a good business plan, and a strong board of directors that represents the community it serves.

In this book, you will learn:
1. What is a nonprofit corporation?
2. Specific rules governing nonprofit boards of directors
3. How to create "fundable" programs and services

4. Basic information about Grants

5. How to entice corporate sponsors/fundraising tips

CHAPTER 1:
What Does "Nonprofit" Mean?

A nonprofit organization is an organization deemed "tax-exempt" by the federal government. In order to get this classification, an organization that intends to operate as a nonprofit must follow a strict application process, which includes business planning and development of a board of directors as well as by-laws, practices, and procedures. State and federal entities also require that some mandatory fees be paid to apply for tax-exempt status.

Nonprofit Classification

An organization is considered a nonprofit when it has received a nonprofit classification from the federal government. There are several classifications, such as religious, educational, business, health, arts, sports, youth, or political. While each type of nonprofit classification has some similarities, some specific guidelines are unique to each classification.

You must understand the type of nonprofit you are part of and the federal rules and guidelines your organization is expected to adhere to. When seeking grant funding, it is essential to look into the types of nonprofits a particular funding entity provides grants to. For instance, some foundations give only to children's programs or religious organizations. There is no point in applying for your sports organization's funding if the grantor only gives to educational nonprofits. Doing research is the key.

Nonprofit Regulation

A nonprofit organization is one that has received tax-exempt status from the federal government. It is regulated by the federal government and must adhere to specific rules, regulations, and reporting practices. In the United States, the Internal Revenue Service carries the burden of monitoring nonprofit organizations' business practices. On a state level, nonprofit organizations are required to keep any nonprofit or fundraising licensing current and file and keep current all Articles of Incorporation.

Acquiring a DUNS Number

Most nonprofit organizations should acquire a DUNS number, which will be used in some business operations. Many grants, specifically those offered via federal and state governments, require each nonprofit to provide a DUNS number when applying for funding. DUNS stands for Data Universal Numbering System, developed by a credit information company, Dun and Bradstreet, in 1962. Acquiring a DUNS number is free and assures the funder that the nonprofit in question is fiscally responsible. The DUNS number can be applied for via the internet at

https://www.dnb.com/duns-number.html.

CHAPTER 2:
Steps to Becoming a Nonprofit Business

The first step to becoming a nonprofit business is to do some significant planning. Most nonprofits are started by a group of community members who notice a specific need in their community. Maybe the community is lacking a comprehensive after school program, or there is a growing homeless population. Perhaps your community has a number of disabled veterans who need some specific services, or maybe, if you live in a large community or urban area, a duplicate organization is required to meet some particular need. In any case, there are particular steps that must be followed when establishing a new nonprofit business, and these steps will take your new nonprofit time to get them accomplished. Taking your new nonprofit from the idea stage to fruition requires some planning, determination, and patience.

The first step is getting like-minded individuals together. You really need to think about this step because it is not just getting the like-minded together. Instead, it is getting like-minded folks who have the time, energy, and commitment, and follow-through together. Having many people sitting in a room merely discussing needs and ideas is not enough to get your business off the ground. It would be best to have people who are willing to work and work for free when your business is starting. It is important to log all those volunteer hours. They have a monetary value when writing grants and looking for funding. So, get yourself a notebook and make sure everyone who helps – including you, the nonprofit's founder – logs every hour they put into getting the new nonprofit off the ground. Every minute counts!

Forming a comprehensive board of directors that is representative of your community is one of the new nonprofit's most significant stepping stones to success. Most founders of a nonprofit position themselves as both the Board President AND the company's Executive Director. However, that is prohibited by the rules and regulations set for nonprofit businesses by the Internal Revenue Service. No board voting board member may profit financially by being a member of the board. Therefore, the Board President and Executive Director are two different positions. Since many nonprofits are forming, the person who will lead the business as the Executive Director acts as the President in the pre-operation stages. Afterward, the position of Board Director is then nominated and voted on by the remaining board members.

It is important to keep your board of directors small but not too small. To begin with, seven is a good number, not to exceed eleven members. Large panels have a more challenging time coming to decisions, so keep it small and the number odd rather than even for voting purposes.

The board is formed of two sections: The Executive Committee and Directors. The Executive Committee consists of the Board President, Vice-President, Secretary, and Treasurer; these members carry the most responsibility for the nonprofit's operations and work hand in hand with the Executive Director. The remaining voting board consists of members known as Directors who help steer the nonprofit's direction and participate in committees and special projects.

Many councils, new and established, may also have a team of Advisors. These are non-voting members that may have some special education, experience, or knowledge and can help the board make informed decisions. It is crucial to choose your board members and advisors wisely, interview each person thoroughly, and make sure the person has the time and commitment to dedicate to the new nonprofit.

Developing a Business Plan

The next step to starting a new nonprofit is to develop a business plan. While many people believe that the first step is to apply for nonprofit status, developing a business plan before applying will make the process easier and your answers to questions regarding the new nonprofit clearer.

As you read further, understand that several of the sections of a business plan require the same information that is required on grant applications – thus, you can see how having this plan in hand will save you a lot of time later when you are applying for funding. Another plus of having a business plan is how that plan helps you market your nonprofit business. Many nonprofits think that they do not have to market or advertise or have a marketing budget because they are nonprofit. However, that is far from the truth. The for-profit businesses need to market to MAKE money. While, the nonprofit businesses must market to RAISE money through awareness of projects, programs, and services and attract donations, grants, corporate sponsors, and endowments.

It is best to divide the parts of the business plan among your board members, each person or committee tackling a section. Assign a due date, and then come together and present the sections. At that point, you can see the "bones" of the business plan and determine what changes, additions, and subtractions the board needs to make. Set another due date to make those changes, then assign a person (preferably someone who has some great organizational – and maybe even some graphic arts skills) to put the plan together. Come together as a board to go over the final draft of the business plan and make sure it looks great.

The parts of a business plan are:

- Executive Summary
- Company Description

7

- Mission Statement
- Business Philosophy
- Ownership of Business
- Goals and Objectives
- Action Plan
- Programs and Services
- Consumers/Clients
- Demographics
- Administrative and Support Team (Staff)
- Marketing Plan
- Competitors
- Financial Information
- Projected Budget

A Word on Mission Statements

The mission statement explains why a particular company exists. It aims to provide an explanation of the company's purpose and how they serve clients. Almost every business is created to cater to specific societal needs, whether that business is a nonprofit organization that provides food to the hungry or a nonprofit that provides gaming and entertainment experiences. Your mission statement will relay the need in your community that your nonprofit meets or fills to the reader.

A solid mission statement must pass across the company's purpose concisely and straightforwardly, both motivational and easy to remember for any company's personnel.

It is a short statement, usually only one sentence (two at the most). The nonprofit's mission statement should contain inspiring words that describe what you do, why you do it, and how you intend to do it. It is a powerful message that makes people want to work with you, come to you for services and programs, donate to you, and volunteer with your organization.

Applying for Nonprofit Status

Application for nonprofit status starts locally (or in-state) and is then accomplished on the federal level. The Internal Revenue Service deals with the regulation of nonprofit businesses in the United States.

After your new board of directors figures out what the new company will be known for, you should then file for a DBA (Doing Business As) in your community. Normally, you would go to your County Clerk's office to accomplish this step, and there is usually a small fee to do so. The County Clerk's office will check to ensure no other business is doing business under the same or a very similar name. Some counties or cities ask you to renew your DBA every year, while others are multi-year. Make sure to check with your local office to find out what their DBA requirements are.

After acquiring your DBA, you will be able to file your Articles of Incorporation with your state. You will go to your state government website to acquire an application, and many will allow you to file online or to FAX your application in. There is a small fee to do this as well. The Articles of Incorporation states your intention to operate as a nonprofit entity. Make a list of who your founders and board of directors are (who is responsible for the business), states your intention to operate as either a membership or non-membership organization, and will ask you to include a copy of your By-Laws.

A word about By-Laws

These no-nonsense rules and regulations state the organization's intention to operate in a professional, business-like, and ethical manner. Many organizations struggle with this document, but in truth, you can find many standard examples of a set of nonprofit By-Laws on the internet and either use a standard example with no changes or alter or edit it to fit your business more closely.

It will take a few weeks to get your official document-stamped Articles of Incorporation back from your state government office. After you receive them, you are an official business and are ready to move forward!

Federal Application for 501c3 Nonprofit Status

In order to apply for your organization's 501c3 tax-exempt status, there are several forms that you are required to file:

IRS Form SS-4: This form allows you to apply for an EIN (Employer Identification Number). The EIN is required for all businesses (not just nonprofit) that employ individuals. You cannot apply for the EIN until the company has been legally formed (DBA and Articles of Incorporation are filed). It does not cost the business anything to submit the SS-4 form, and it can be done online at **www.irs.gov** or by calling toll free (866) 816-2065 in the United States.

IRS Form 1023: This form provides the Internal Revenue Service with a comprehensive look at your prospective business. You will be able to use the business plan you created to help answer some of the questions on the form. The 1023 form will also ask that you submit a projected budget for the organization. The user fee for Form 1023 to apply for nonprofit status is $600. If the budget is expected to be more than $40,000, the fee to apply for nonprofit status is $700. The fee must be paid through **Pay.gov** during application and is nonrefundable.

Depending on the type of nonprofit you are starting, some other required federal forms may fill out. However, most nonprofits simply fill out IRS forms SS-4 and 1023.

After applying, it will take several months for the application to be reviewed by the Internal Revenue Service and a determination be made.

License to Solicit Charitable Funds

Another form that must be filed on a state level is the License to Solicit Charitable Funds. In most states, filing this form is free; however, some states may charge a nominal fee. Most states require this form to be renewed each year. It allows the organization to do fundraising work and events and to solicit grant funds.

Now that you have all the paperwork completed, the most challenging task of waiting begins. In the meantime, there is still work your newly formed board of directors can get done. Let's move on!

CHAPTER 3:
Developing Programs and Services

Waiting for the 501c3 tax-exempt determination letter from the Internal Revenue Service is probably the most challenging part of the process of starting a new nonprofit business. However, while you and your new board of directors are waiting, you should be doing some critical planning and implementation for the organization.

Developing a plan for the programs and services offered by the organization is imperative prior to the launch of the business. There are several steps to developing this plan, and it is quite possible that you may have completed some of the research that is required. In fact, that is probably where your great idea for the new nonprofit came from, seeing a specific need in the community, and researching that need.

Look at your mission statement and think about the reason your new nonprofit will exist. Think about the specific population of people it will serve. What does your target audience desire? How will the new organization lead to a better quality of life for the people it will serve? What kinds of programs or help will it provide?

When you look at the answers to these questions, it will help you determine many things: how large of a facility will the organization need for its operations and facilitation of programs and services? How many and what type of staff will you have to hire? Will any of those staff require special licensing or certifications? What will the salary requirements for those employees be? What types of materials, supplies, or equipment will be required in order to provide those programs and services?

Perhaps a crucial question to ask yourself is how you will evaluate the nonprofit's programs and services to determine their success in helping the specific population or populations the organization serves?

Evaluation is the most ignored and possibly the most crucial component of program planning. When requesting a grant, funders want to know how you will determine: (a) the success of the program or project, (b) were any program components unsuccessful, (c) who is in charge of reviews, (d) how does the organization utilize the info? Evaluation tools are available in different formats.

Discuss with your community partners to find out what types they have used, what works well, and what doesn't. Some agencies hire an evaluation service to formally document statistics and interpret them.

It would be best for your organization to create a sub-committee which is dedicated to the assessment of the programs and services offered by your nonprofit business. The said committee is responsible for conducting research on different evaluation tools and methods. They should also come up with a way to gather data, assemble it, and make formal reports one to two times a year.

This is a very useful material for reporting to grantors when seeking grant funding. The information is a great marketing tool for your organization, which helps to show how much impact you make on your clients as well as the community.

Consider Your Potential Consumers

One of your greatest assets when planning your services and programs are the folks you intend to serve. Reaching out to these potential clients to find out their specific needs will help you formulate a successful program. Find out how their needs have been met in the past – both successfully and unsuccessfully. Where they have gone for help, and what kinds of assistance are lacking.

Potential consumers can be a wealth of information when planning programs and services. They are also potential volunteers, committee members and can sit as advisors on your board of directors. Who better to know what types of programs and services are needed, and what will work or not work than the people who need them? Reaching out to some potential consumers who are excited about the prospect of new services and programs in their community is a great way to give your new nonprofit a leg up when in the planning stages.

Community Partners

Another essential part of developing programs and services is to network in your community and establish a list of community partners. These may be other nonprofit and for-profit businesses, churches, schools, governmental agencies, or philanthropic entities who may have a vested interest in your nonprofit and the services it will provide in the community. Perhaps representatives from some of these agencies and organizations may fill a seat on your board of directors or act as advisors. Perhaps it is a charitable organization that has promised funding to your organization. A community partner is a person or organization that gives help or assistance to your organization in some form. Establishing community partners is an integral part of the nonprofit's operation. It is when many hands join together in a community that we can make great things happen.

CHAPTER 4:
Applying for Grants – A Brief Overview

Application Types

There are a few types of grant applications to be aware of. Never ignore the type and format of the grant application requested by the granting organization. Grants that are not properly formatted will likely not be reviewed, thus wasting your time and energy. Not to mention, it will not get your nonprofit organization the funding it needs. These application types are:

- Full Proposal
- Letter proposal
- Form Proposal
- Online Application
- Proposal Plus Presentation

Parts of a Grant

The Executive Summary: While the Executive Summary is the first section of each grant, it is best to write this section last. It is a brief statement that describes the organization, the reason you are seeking grant dollars, and why you believe a partnership between your organization and the potential funder is a good fit. This section, usually only half a page to one page in length, will describe the grant proposal's highlights.

Mission and History: This section will contain your organization's mission statement, as stated in the nonprofit's Articles of Incorporation. It is also necessary to include a brief history of the organization. Beginning with its inception up to the present. Who are the organization's beneficiaries (and how many), where it is located, and its growth over time.

Statement of Need: The Statement of Need is going to incorporate some hard data – statistics, which prove why your nonprofit organization and the programs and services you provide are essential to your community – specifically the particular population you serve such as homeless people, out of school youth, abused women and children, etc.)

Goals, Objectives, and Outcomes: A goal is an abstract, intangible statement that states what your program or project intends to accomplish, while an objective is a specific statement that is bound to a time frame. Prospective grantors want to be assured that you are setting goals and objectives for your program or project and that you are anticipating some specific outcomes. An outcome is the end product of the objective.

Timetable for Implementation: Most grant awards are time-sensitive; therefore, grantors usually request a timeframe for implementation on their grant applications. In this section, you will map the duration of the program or project, when it will start, when and if it will end. Some programs are ongoing. In this case, that should be stated in the timeframe and the ways your organization intends to fund the program in the future.

Community Need/Resources: When you are seeking funding, a grantor will likely ask your organization if your programs provide a "replication of services" in the community. This would also mean that the grantor requires additional information on other nonprofits or companies in your area that offer similar services.

Target Recipients of the Nonprofit: Grantors would often ask for demographic information that describes the individuals your nonprofit provides service to. The data information about your target population is can be found on uscensus.org if you are searching for statistics on households, sex, race, size of families, income, etc.

Staff Training, Education, and Expected Certifications: In this section, you will document the knowledge, education, and experience of your administrators and staff. You can gather all the information needed from the resumes and any certifications that your administrators and staff have provided your company.

Program Sustainability: It is important for your nonprofit to draft (and follow) a three to five-year sustainability plan and to share it with your potential funders. Most grantors would want to know how your business will survive beyond grant awards. Many companies organize fundraisers in their local communities, find corporate donors, and establish endowments from supporters. Some nonprofits may provide fee-based services, while others (like an organization that assist the physically challenged) may seek federal or state contracts that pay, in part, for the services the nonprofit provides. Showing the grantor all the ways the nonprofit has the potential to bring in revenue doesn't mean you don't need a grant. It simply demonstrates that your organization is responsible and that you are thinking about the future of your nonprofit and its sustainability.

Required Attachments

Grantors have a common list of required attachments that you must send along with your grant applications. These attachments include:

- Copy of current IRS determination letter (501c3)
- List of Board of Directors with affiliations
- Most recent audit
- Most recent 990 (IRS)
- Letters of Support

- Annual Report (if available)

Drafting the Cover Letter

A cover letter must be provided to show courtesy at the beginning of any grant proposal. The cover letter should be straightforward; introducing your nonprofit and the reason you are applying for the grant. The cover letter can mirror the Executive Summary found at the beginning of the grant. Always thank the foundation or giving corporation at the end of the cover letter for giving your company the opportunity to apply for funding.

_____

For more detailed information about grant writing, also check out the book: **How To Write A Nonprofit Grant Proposal: Writing Winning Proposals To Fund Your Programs And Projects**

CHAPTER 5:
What Do Grantors Look For?

There are many private, philanthropic organizations that invest money to generate interest that is used to provide grant funding for nonprofit entities. Philanthropic organizations must, by law, give away five percent of their interest earnings per year. Those interest earnings equal grant dollars.

In the 1900s, there were lots of grant funds available, both private and governmental, but as the nation's economy began to struggle, many funds dried up, and grants became more and more competitive. Hence, it is essential to pinpoint what funders look for when applying for grant monies.

One of the most important factors that potential grantors look at is the sustainability of an organization. Gone are the days when a nonprofit business can survive on grant funding alone. Philanthropic organizations like to see that the prospective grantee has an excellent financial plan and that it is working to raise its own operations revenue via fundraising events, memberships, contracts, and endowments and fees for programs and services. A question that is often asked during the grant-seeking process is, "How will the organization facilitate this program if it does not receive 100% of the funding requested?"

This is an important question that showcases your commitment to the potential program, service, or project. Are you committed enough to find a way to deliver the proposed project, program, or service even if you do not receive the grant? Essentially, do you have a Plan B?

Another aspect grantors look at is the longevity of the organization that is applying. Local and private funders are a bit more lenient on this factor; however, most state and federal funders like to grant funds to organizations that have been operating successfully for at least three years. Many new nonprofits are developed believing that there are myriads of state and federal funds available – and it is true that there are quite a lot of these types of grants out there – however, a track record of successful operations is key in acquiring these types of grants.

Financial transparency is another aspect of a nonprofit's operations that a potential grantor looks at. Transparency means that information about the nonprofit organization's financial position, how and where the money is spent, where the money is generated from, accounting practices, how the organization is financially managed and governed is readily available. Transparency also speaks of the organization's provision of services, hiring and firing, and its clients' or consumers' satisfaction.

Essentially, a potential grantor likes to be assured that the organization they are considering giving funding to is responsible, ethical, and financially sound. A grantor wants to invest in an organization that is successful, so be sure to follow ethical business and accounting practices and document everything.

CHAPTER 6:
Seeking Corporate Sponsorships

Another source of large donations and grants are corporate sponsors. Most large enterprises have community programs where the corporation's employees invest for the good of the community in which it operates. Some larger corporations, such as Ford Motor Company and General Electric, and DuPont, give global levels. It is possible to apply for grants from larger corporations, whether or not that corporation has a presence in your community; however, those grants are difficult to attain.

When seeking corporate funding and donations, it is most important to network with the specific corporations you wish to engage in. Get to know the company through research and community events. Invite potential corporate sponsors to visit your organization, even participate as volunteers. You want them to see the good works before reaching out to them for grant funds or donations. You want to entice them to want to give to your organization before you apply.

Corporate sponsors will be looking for the very same things a philanthropic organization does: good business practices, financial transparency, satisfied clients and consumers, and a good reputation in the community. Corporate sponsors want to invest in success and an organization with an excellent track record.

Some corporate sponsors have a granting process similar to that of philanthropic organizations, requiring a formal application. Others ask that your nonprofit visits, often attend a board meeting, give a presentation about your organization, and submit a request for funding or a donation. Some will act as a sponsor for a large fundraising event or give to a specific project, such as the purchase or construction of a new building, purchase of equipment, or "adopt" a particular program of the nonprofit. Corporate sponsors are, if not more, important as grant funders. Generally, corporate sponsors operate in your community and therefore have a vested interest in the success, safety, and growth of that community. It is imperative that you engage businesses in your community, large and small, and invite them to be a part of your nonprofit organization, its programs, and projects.

CHAPTER 7:
Steps to Hosting A Successful Annual Campaign

STEP 1: Create a Steering Committee

A campaign steering committee is a group of people that lead and plan an Annual Campaign until a permanent committee is in place.

STEP 2: Plan Campaign

A good and solid campaign should be in place before you start soliciting donors or gifts, and even volunteers. The plan should always include a budget, a timeline, an organizational chart, a range of gift tables, and financial or gift accounting procedures.

STEP 3: Recruit Campaign Team

The next important thing to do after the organization has a plan is to identify campaign leadership. Leadership is crucial when it comes to the success of an Annual Campaign. A leader can singlehandedly determine the success or the failure of an Annual Campaign.

One of the best criteria for selecting a leader is to recruit a campaign leader from outside the organization's governing board. Including volunteers from outside the board will allow the organization to broaden its reach within the community.

Selecting a leader outside the organization's governing board will also provide the community with an incentive that the campaign's goal is to provide a fundraising effort and not just oppose another fundraiser.

STEP 4: Develop Marketing Strategy

It would help if you don't focus the campaign on the money; instead, your focus should be on the money. The campaign's marketing material should be focused on addressing the needs of the community and communicating the impact of the organization.

Essential components of every marketing strategy must encompass the campaign theme, case statements, collateral media, and internal and external campaign events. Also, include an appropriate budget for the media services.

The marketing strategy should be comprehensive and should be designed to highlight the importance of making a gift to the organization.

STEP 5: Conduct Internal Campaign

The foundation of the entire Annual Campaign is based on the board campaign (Internal Gifts). The ultimate endgame of the Internal Gifts Campaign is full participation. You can't get any form of support from the community until your organization has achieved 100% board giving from the Board of Directors.

STEP 6: Conduct External Prospect ID & Rating

The principal goal here is to create a comprehensive prospect list right before external solicitations begin. Making this list before the tenders will allow your organization to conduct the external solicitations in an orderly manner. This means the prospects that can give the most will be solicited first. This way, momentum can easily be generated by focusing on the more prominent donors first.

STEP 7: Conduct External Campaign

A lot of positioning and planning has been done for months at this point in the Annual Campaign process. After the campaign marketing strategy goes live, and various committees (including non-board members) have been recruited, and most importantly, there is a 100% participation in the Internal Gifts Campaign. At this point, the external prospect list has also been sufficiently developed to support the campaign. With all these, you are now ready to state your case for the community support at large and secure the required funds for your organization.

STEP 8: Evaluate Campaign

Analyzing is very important when it comes to any process. It is crucial to take your time while making decisions that involve the Annual Campaign. You should examine the results of the campaign, and you should also identify specific weaknesses and strengths. All this information will be relevant when making plans for the next campaign.

STEP 9: Conduct Ongoing Cultivation & Stewardship
To get the best results, organizations should make fundraising an ongoing approach through stewardship and cultivation. Try not to view your successful campaign at the end of your campaign. Instead, make it the beginning of a new relationship.

Successful fundraising should be based on the successful connection you have made with donors and the emotional bond they've created with your organization.

Cultivating requires you to foster the growth of something, and in this case, the support for your organization is the "something."

As an organization, you need a plan on how to cultivate new and existing donors. The critical point is to create as much connection as possible with your organization and your donor.

Stewardship is defined as responsible and careful management of things that are entrusted to one's care. When it comes to the Annual Campaign, it means the donors are entrusting their financial investment with your organization. It is now your sole responsibility to manage those gifts in the way they were intended and give a concise report of your donors' investments.

Stewardship and cultivation are an efficient way to make your Board of Directors active in fundraising success for your organization. Although most board members aren't comfortable asking for money, some might still be willing to meet with donors and prospects to discuss your organization.

CHAPTER 8:
Conducting an Annual Nonprofit Campaign

It is understandable to have some reservations about hosting an Annual Campaign, but there is no reason you should not conduct a campaign. You should conduct an Annual Campaign even:

- If your organization is relatively new
- If your organization has gone public
- If you have a vast organization
- Or, if your organization is minimal.

With the above, you should know that you are eligible to conduct an Annual Campaign, no matter the size of your organization. In my experience, various organizations have found different excuses not to conduct a campaign, one of them being "our community is different."

Most of these excuses will keep your organization from growing and prevent your organization from attaining its proactive mode of development and keeping you reactive. The idea of having an Annual Campaign can be daunting and overwhelming.

This book will reveal some important reasons why you should conduct an Annual Campaign.

Annual Campaign, as a term, can be applied in different ways. In this book, "Annual Campaign" will be defined as an appeal that searches for unrestricted operating funds from their primarily individual donors, corporations, and foundations. It will also be interpreted as a board-driven fundraising effort.

I believe it is critical to sit down and research places where the money comes from when it comes to seeking gifts and annual campaigns. Below is a chart that shows the statistics of how money is donated to foundations and campaigns.

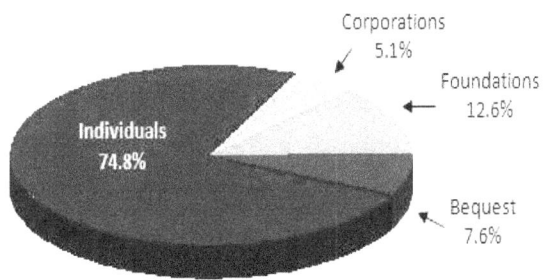

Source: Giving USA Foundation™ – Giving USA 2008

The Annual Campaign will provide you an opportunity to receive funds and individual target donors from the donor group, which might be difficult to reach without a campaign.

Before you start a campaign, it is crucial to understand that most of the solicitations will be directed towards individuals since they make up the largest segment of the pie chart (the donor population). Now that we have established the location of the funds, it is time to discuss the various reasons why your organization should organize an Annual Campaign.

Sell the Mission

The Annual Campaign gives your organization an opportunity to sell your goals. Most of the time, small nonprofit organizations tend to create a society of ticket buyers and not the planned community of investors or donors.

Some organizations sell raffle tickets, nonprofits sell tickets to a Gala, and others tend to sell a quartet for a golf course. Most of these groups make good sales, yet they usually claim it's for the community's betterment.

With these experiences and opportunities, most ticket buyers or 'donors' won't be able to make a deep connection to the vision or the mission of the organization. They play in the tournament, and sometimes they'll have dinner and toss away their tickets. They'll never really have the chance to learn about the work of the organization and the various good that the organization has done for the society.

The Annual Campaign instead gives the organization a chance for the clients to meet with their host, their program, and, most importantly, their goals. Personal solicitations will provide the organization a chance to convince the donor for unrestricted gifts.

The solicitations will also give the donor the opportunity to learn about the importance of making donations and gifts, and the value of those gifts to the community. When the donor fully understands the impact, mission, and reason for support, the goal for organizing the Annual Campaign has been achieved.

Move donors up the giving pyramid

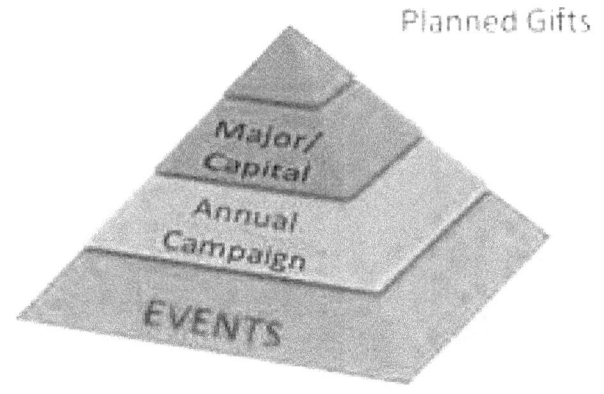

Taking the time to connect donors with your goals and missions at your Annual Campaign gives you and your organizations a chance to move the donor pyramid upward. Take a good look at the diagram upwards, and you will discover that 'events' are located at the bottom with the red color. The events are primarily where the donor enters the giving cycle.

There are often people that'll attend the event to make a donor and sometimes to represent an organization. When the person attends, it is now your sole responsibility you make the casual attendee to an annual donor. This requires stewardship and cultivation.

When you have now converted the attendee to an annual donor, the next important step is to cultivate a meaningful relationship with him/her. As the donors' relationship with the organization improves with time, the donor will eventually become a major or capital donor that might hopefully make a planned gift to the organization in the nearest future.

A planned gift is the ultimate goal for any development. Most of the time, individuals make a planned gift to organizations that they feel close to and whom they've made a deep connection with. Donors usually don't jump from being an attendee to a planned gift donor; it is typically a process that takes time and energy to foster relationships and moving up the pyramid sequentially.

Your organization's goal is to move all of your donors up the giving pyramid until they reach the planned gift section. The Annual Campaign provides the perfect avenue to do just that and more.

Cost-Effective
The cost associated with the Annual Campaign is minimal because the campaign relies on face to face

solicitations. You don't need to splurge on expensive solicitation packets. All your organization need is intent to pledge or give forms and a carefully outlined case statement.

Unlike many events requiring organizations to spend up to $60 per attendee, the Annual Campaign does not need these expenses and makes space for more gifts to be attained by the organization. A board also directs the Annual Campaign; therefore, organizations that work with non-existent development teams should still be able to conduct a campaign.

Why Not?

Is there any reason why organizations shouldn't give individuals from their community a chance to invest in their business or organization? Both staff members and board members should feel great about the service they're rendering to their environment and are likely proud of their organization.

In this case, they will be pleased to invite their neighbors to give and invest. Fundraising can be a little of both science and art with one constant fact; If your organization doesn't ask for gifts, it won't receive gifts.

I hope you're now ready to begin an annual campaign after reading this chapter! The advantages you get from starting a yearly campaign is far more than the disadvantages. If your organization is looking to move to the next level, then an Annual Campaign is essential.

The campaign will give the organization a chance to stay on its goals and, at the same, time meet potential investors and develop meaningful relationships with them. This will lead to the long term sustainability and success of the organization.

CHAPTER 9:

Using Social Networking Technologies in Your Nonprofit Organization

Social networking has become the new trend for nonprofit organizations since the political campaign of former President Barack Obama. A lot of money was raised, and millions of people participated in arguably one of the best movements in the modern world.

Executives and boards are now asking, "Is there a way to reincarnate what Senator Barack Obama did to move millions of volunteers and raise money from different new sources?"

An increasingly popular avenue for nonprofits to raise income is fundraising. And social media has been a form of a gold mine for nonprofit organizations that are into fundraising. However, most people are not able to generate more than a few dollars!

A lot of people are familiar with the online campaigning platform called "Causes." At this moment, up to 25 million people around the world have joined at least a particular Cause with the website. Up to 230,000 nonprofit organizations use the platform. The numbers are high, but check this, less than one percent of the population makes donations through the website.

The largest organization in the Cause app has over 5 million users and raised only $50,000. The average of these numbers means only one cent is donated per member! This does not account for the volunteer and staff to raise the money. At this moment, this source is not the solution to all your fundraising needs.

The important thing is understanding the value of Twitter, Instagram, Facebook, and other social networking sites in communicating with people, keeping them informed about what you do, and educating them about your organization. These technologies allow you to stay in touch with your constituents (volunteers, donors, staff, clients, etc.) and meet new people – building relationships and cultivation.

The principles of effective and successful fundraising are the same online as it has always been, "People giving gifts to other people."

Organizations should take this to practice while using social media and networking. The only level of success can be acquired through untargeted mail campaigns and cold calls when it comes to communicating from unknown sources.

Word of mouth will be more effective because of the personal credibility that is established through personal relationships. Engage all your volunteers, the organization's staff, and other members of the process. Show them the required information and ask them to disseminate it appropriately.

Start Conversations
One of the most significant changes made by the progress in social networking in organizations is the change in cumbersome communication to a simpler conversational mode of communication. Most of the time, organizations have published reports, newsletters, and others to volunteers, donors, and some other community members. This is still quite important.

Although, with the use of social networking, the organization will get ideas, feedback, and opinions from its constituents. Organizations that tend to change their culture to this source will engage constituents more actively, deepen their relationship, and are better informed about the perception of the organization and your community needs. These changes are essential for most organizations moving forward.

Think About Other Uses of Social Networking
Apart from the development goals of your organization, there are also other various benefits you can get from social networking. For example, technologies are used for both nonprofits and productive purposes to improve

the sharing of information and the development of new skills around the organization.

A concise survey by the MASIE Center claims more than 1,000 professionals realize that most organizations use social learning: Social technology and social networks for crucial organizational learning outcomes. Up to 60% of all the respondents said social education is valuable.

Make a Plan!
- Create a budget. Make sure it includes both indirect and direct costs, such as software.
- Identify networks and technologies that you will use to connect and form a meaningful relationship with people.
- Be sure of your objectives. Find your potential market. Find the number of people in your community that are likely to use social media? What percentage can you attract to your network? How will you benefit from your relationships with them? Volunteers? Donations? Awareness? Don't forget internal uses like sharing expertise, and information within the organization by the board, volunteers, staff, etc.?
- Identify the cost of creating content and skills involved in conveying with people. Don't forget, it is an ongoing investment that takes skills and time.

CHAPTER 10:
Social Networking for Nonprofit Organizations

Social networks like Instagram, YouTube, Twitter, LinkedIn, Facebook, and others had created an excitement that is the same as when Hotmail changed email from an ordinary business tool to an essential part of people's lives. Social networking has now become the talk of the town.

Also, a vast number of people are using technology to connect with their friends, colleagues, and families. According to estimates, there are up to 243.6 million social network American users as of 2019. Imagine how this number would increase in the next decade.

Important executives in different organizations noticed when former President Obama used YouTube, Facebook, Instagram, and social blogs to build a massive amount of volunteers, workers, and supporters. His unique use of social media helped former President Barack Obama raise unprecedented funds and transformed political campaigning.

The million dollars question from managers and boards all over the world is, "How do we replicate what Former

President Obama did and control millions of volunteers to raise funds from new sources?

Lessons Learned from the Obama Campaign
Let's take a brief moment to define social networking before moving to the lessons and information acquired from the former president's presidential campaign. To be concise, a social network can be defined as a collection of individuals and organizations that come together to share their likes and interests.

There are many forms of this on the Internet, and including collaborative content creation, blogs, business networks, email blasts, and socializing.

The presidential campaign of former president Obama mobilized up to 3 million people on MySpace and Facebook combined (this is thrice the number reported for Senator John McCain's campaign), many of which became evangelists and volunteers for his campaign. Former President Obama campaign is also reported to have raised upwards of $600 million, with the majority of these donations made online. With up to 16 different social networks, he made sure his followers were continuously updated.

The Obama campaign gave President Obama an edge over all of his competitions. He became a charismatic leader and a celebrity among people. He made sure that his message was delivered to the highly political scene. Most of his supporters were young people that were highly interested; they were also the most active demographic in the social media network.

A presidential campaign has a wide range of volunteers, donors, and potential voters to target. He also had a 24-hour coverall that kept sound bites, stories, images, and opinions, which were sent to the streets, workplaces, home, and the likes.

The rockstar personality portrayed by former President Barack Obama was not the only reason for the success of his campaign. One of his strategic objectives was to make Obama campaign a channel to connect with his supporters.

It had the endorsement and support of the highest level of the campaign, including former President Barack Obama himself. A lot of money and time was allocated to social media, and the campaign maintained a detailed and highly focused approach to managing its use of social media networking.

So what about social networking and nonprofits?
A lot of nonprofits want what former President Barack Obama has achieved. These include a large number of engaged support, network effects, and widespread awareness, a cheap way to reach many people, many donors, driving them to a particular goal, and collecting money and gifts from them.

But you have to be realistic. Most nonprofits don't have a celebrity, charismatic leader, even on the local market. Having celebrities to support your organization is not similar to having one that is the center of your organization.

The numbers of the Obama campaign showed that he extensively used MySpace, and Facebook to reach many users. But that amount in absolute numbers is only a few percentage points of the total number of the user base. Therefore, even if a nonprofit organization was able to reach the percentage of users similar to the Obama campaign, the reach will still be quite small.

Social media is not a pot of gold for fundraising. Although it is potentially valuable and useful in many ways that include:

- Fundraising is a very crucial first step in relationship building and cultivation.
- Establish a secure and cost-effective way to engage awareness.
- Connecting with clients and other stakeholders.
- Listen more to your clients and stakeholders, even if it means shifting your culture.
- Change your communication to a conversational mode instead of the usual one-way approach of most communications.
- Keep an open mind! Look at Facebook, which started just in 2004. Now, it has millions of users globally.

- Learn something about social networking, what it is, who uses it, and how it works.
- Talk to people. Learn about people's personal experiences and how they operate their business. Try to pick their brain to know what they know, what works, and what doesn't. If they use social media for business, check or measure how much benefit social networking has provided for them.
- Do it! Try to open a social media account for yourself on Twitter, Instagram, and Facebook. I suggest you ask some of your friends about the kinds of social media they have, then try and open an account for yourself. You will quickly become part of their conversations. Learn how it works, what can be beneficial, and the result of the whole experiment.

Use Common Sense

When it comes to Internet technologies, some social media sites are targeted by different malware forms like viruses. It would be best if you used smart technologies like anti-virus to prevent viruses from entering your phone. You should also be careful of people you share confidential information about your organization and yourself with.

Important New Way to Do Business

Social media networking is as good as you've heard. It is a vital tool for doing business and will continue to remain valuable for organizations and individuals that chose to understand and invest in its possibilities.

CHAPTER 11:
Planning a Special Nonprofit Event

When it comes to special events, you either hate them or like them. Either way, if you're a nonprofit organization, you will likely conduct this kind of events throughout the whole year.

The events may be public relations, for your program participants, or even fundraising. Regardless of the reason(s) for the event, some basic principles and rules are available to make your event more enjoyable and less painful.

An important theme in this book is about keeping your events upbeat and lively. Some key points about special events are excitement, motivation, and fun associated with such activities. Whether it is a carnival at the park, a fundraising breakfast, or you're having a formal gala, the participants of these events must have a wonderful experience for the events to be successful.

When it comes to event planning, the Animation Plan is handy. The Animation Plan is the programmer's vision of the program in terms of the way participants move and experience the events.

The Animation Plan should include any of these components:

1. Name of Event - a clever and catchy name should be created for the event
2. Time
3. Location
4. Date
5. Goal and Description of Event - when the event comes to an end, what is the desired outcome?
6. Timeline for task completion - List all tasks
7. Execute the tasks
8. Schedule of Events - ends with a clean-up and set-up
9. Crowd Control / Behavior Control
10. Leader/Volunteer Responsibilities and Orientation
11. Description of Attendees - volunteers, the general public, organization participants, and donors.
12. Closing
13. Clean-up
14. Possible Problems - anticipate any potential problems
15. Description of Activities – Make a list of every activity that will occur during the special event and get a detailed description of the activities that will happen (for example: registration, cocktail hour, auctions, etc.)

16. Risk Management Plan involves the following:

- Policies/Procedures
- Activities
- Facility
- Equipment
- Layout

Apart from the above items, it would help if you created a flowchart for the events. The flowchart must be simple and must reflect a significant milestone for planning events in concert with the calendar.

The Animation Plan should be comprehensive and thorough. Imagine if you're the one planning an event, and you suddenly fell bed-ridden or sick on the day of the event.

An average person without the knowledge of the event should be able to use the Animation Plan to deliver and understand the event. It should be detailed! Step-by-step, scenario by scenario!

This Animation Plan:
- Allows for continuity (makes event reproducible)
- Identifies problems
- Serves as an evaluation tool
  Pushes the planner to plan ahead
- Provides direction for staff and volunteers

- Provides documentation of the event, which can reduce legal liability.

Now that you have a solid plan for the execution of the special event, you can now focus on the critical things that'll make the event truly "special."

Here are only a few ideas and tips that can make your event truly successful. A comprehensive, well-thought plan will help in the execution and delivery of the event. The plan will also help to reduce stress for volunteers and planners.

CHAPTER 12:
Board Recruitment for Nonprofit Organizations

The truth is both staff and volunteers are responsible for developing, recruiting, and identifying volunteer leaders for your organization. Also, each group needs to take various steps to move the process to a successful conclusion.

It is widely accepted that it is the job of the staff to develop a particular 'wish list' of the individuals that should be part of the board's volunteers in your organization. You can easily do this by identifying and examining the need of the board for various areas of expertise and the people with influence in your area.

After the development of the wish list, the next important thing for staff is to review the list with the board development committee to make sure that those chosen are the perfect candidate for your organization.

Nobody should be placed on the list without the approval of the committee, and you should never approach anybody for board involvement without passing through the process of agreement and identification that they are indeed the perfect candidate for the board position.

After the list has been scrutinized and developed, your staff should do research about every individual on the list. Essential parts of the research should include volunteer involvement, educational background, business relationships, giving history, and giving capacity, etc.

Your organization should develop a strategy to determine the best person to approach the individual for his/her service. The staff is responsible for preparing volunteers identified as the best individual for recruitment and the materials required to help the volunteer with his presentation during recruitment.

Teams should also be on call to help any volunteers when there is a need for it, and the volunteer might not be able to answer. The need usually arises when information is being asked about the kind of service your organization provides, which the volunteer may not be able to afford.

After the recruitment has been successful, the staff's responsibility is to set the volunteers to work. This involves projects that might work throughout the year, committee involvement, potential supporters that could be solicited during the campaign process, and personal giving to the organization.

The board members are also responsible for assisting the volunteers with engagement, making sure they feel welcomed on the board, and encouraging them to be involved in events and meetings.

If properly executed, the process will move towards making sure your board is provided with the perfect plan for your nonprofit organization.

Conclusion

As you can see, starting a new nonprofit takes a lot of work and dedication. But, know that every contribution you can make to your community is the pot at the end of the rainbow.

It is amazing to see how the good ideas and hearts of a few dedicated people can work together for a community's social benefit. Remember, planning is the key, then following through to achieve your goals.

Best of luck in your new nonprofit venture!

.